And the Wretched

And the Wretched

Narayan Sahoo

Translated by
Sanjeet Kumar Das

BLACK EAGLE BOOKS
Dublin, USA | Bhubaneswar, India

Black Eagle Books
USA address:
  7464 Wisdom Lane
Dublin, OH 43016

India address:
E/312, Trident Galaxy, Kalinga Nagar,
Bhubaneswar-751003, Odisha, India

E-mail: info@blackeaglebooks.org
Website: www.blackeaglebooks.org

First International Edition Published by
Black Eagle Books, 2024

AND THE WRETCHED
by **Narayan Sahoo**

Translated by **Sanjeet Kumar Das**

Original Copyright © Narayan Sahoo
Translation Copyright © Sanjeet Kumar Das

All rights reserved. No part of this publication may be reproduced, stored in a retrieval system, or transmitted, in any form or by any means, electronic, mechanical, photocopying, recording or otherwise without the prior permission of the publisher.

Cover & Interior Design: Ezy's Publication

ISBN- 978-1-64560-526-3 (Paperback)
Library of Congress Control Number: 2024933737

Printed in the United States of America

*For Swopna, My Daughter
Sujata, My Wife and
Bapa and Maa*

And the Wretched: A Literary Evaluation

Prof. Narayan Sahoo is a renowned doyen of the Odia literature. His play *Bewildered God* deeply moved his readers and audience, who loved to watch dramas. His most influential work, *And the Wretched*, was broadcast on All India Radio, staged by the actors of different drama institutes and well-appreciated by the populace all over Odisha.

The poor and the downtrodden have been oppressed and subdued in society for ages. Forever, they tolerate injustice, atrocity, harassment and exploitation of the dominant class, which is hegemonic in different social spheres. Lazy, unenterprising, non-reactive, and lacking self-confidence, the oppressed have decided to stand last as their natural religion, and they will stick to it. They don't have the power and courage to come to the front. It's their luck to bear the burden of social oppression and injustice for many years. Based on this social-realistic thought, the play *And the Wretched* is scripted. The theme describes its background in the Brechtian epic style of writing the play. This play humbly inaugurates the naked truth of socio-economic-political oppression of the socially unprivileged class experiences, citing instances from mythology, history and contemporary society.

Those who had participated and fought bravely against the most influential British Government day and night imagined that they would see India as an exploitation-free golden country after independence. However, after independence, there was a creation of a privileged class. This group trickily acquired political and authoritative power. Those who made a lot of sacrifices, having been deeply absorbed in the spirit of Nationalism, were kept aloof. The rich, the landlords, the capitalists, the business tycoons, the politicians, the bureaucrats and the heads of different religious institutes started to expand their dominance in other social domains. Because of these powerful groups, the poor and the disadvantaged groups suffered incessantly over the years socially, economically, politically and religiously. The gap between the poor and the rich gradually widened. The sorrows and sufferings of the downtrodden and the exploited were devoid of feelings. This play is what the present lifestyle of contemporary India is about. This background issue brings the playwright's central message to the limelight. To strengthen the principal thought, the playwright has displayed the stories enshrined in the great epic of India, *the Mahabharat*, and the pages of history.

The play revolves around realistic social thought. The revolutionary attempt of the playwright against social injustice and exploitation is brought in the best possible manner through this text. The oppressed get reawakened and strengthened to fight against the social oddities. They are empowered and motivated to voice and stand against society's unjust system. Towards the end of the play, this voice reverberates, "Taking advantage of your weakness and putting their legs upon you, they stepped up higher and higher. It bothers me when you don't raise your voice.

For how many days will you stay like this? Try to wake up and revitalize the power that is within you." (page.34)

The Aryans have always subdued and tortured the non-Aryans diachronically. Of course, the tribes have repeatedly opposed and united to raise their voice against the social system. When they are assaulted, they have reacted vehemently against the bad practices of the society. They are not afraid of life. They have decided to safeguard their life and are conscious of their self-respect. One scene of the *Mahabharat* is considered and described in the first part of the play. When unjust Durjyodhan and his brothers, unable to realize the consequences, attempt to rape Jara Shabar's wife, they are vigorously assaulted by Jara. The brave Jara have shot arrows at all the Kaurav brothers, keeping in view giving the devils their due for their short-sightedness. All of them have lost their consciousness. But the incident followed after that is sensitive. The moment Guru Dronacharya has reached the spot, he is aware of the extraordinary power of Jara. He thinks that all the Pandav-Kaurav bravery is dim and powerless before Jara. The science of arms he taught the princes will be in vain. Because of simplicity, Jara confesses that he has indirectly learnt this science from Guru Drona.

When Guru requests Jara to restore life to the dead bodies, he effortlessly converts vitality in them. Then, the unparalleled hero is trapped in the conspiracy of Guru and faces the extreme downfall of his life. In the name of *Guru Dakshina* Ekalavya (also known as Jara), following the instructions of Guru, he cuts his thumb of his right hand. For all the times after that, he loses his power to shoot the arrows. An archer second to none, Ekalavya becomes an ordinary archer because of Guru Drona's heinous cheating.

Jara or Ekalavya represents the tribal non-Aryan community, while Guru Drona represents the Aryan community of city life. Nowadays, the tribes are exploited and susceptible to the conspiracies the civilized city people set.

The subsequent representation concerns the Sun Temple construction and its history in the play. King Narasingh Dev has imagined the temple to be stood and worshipped for ages as one of the monumental creations of human civilization. By the decree of the King, twelve hundred sculptors work hard day and night and, in the end, are carved the beautiful designs of fine arts in the temple. Thinking of the severe punishment, they have forgotten their proper food for twelve years, their livelihood; after all, they have forgotten their families, parents, wives and children. In the meantime, some sculptors become weak, and some die. Their families are suffering from a massive financial crisis.

At last, the King's wish gets fulfilled, and his flag of glory is hoisted everywhere. The excessive exploitation of the workers lurking beneath the background of the Sun Temple is not visible to the world. The outstanding work of King Narasingh Dev pleases all. But the agonies and sufferings (both physical and mental) of the sculptors have never been fore-grounded. Nobody questions them at all.

The third part of the play depicts contemporary political exploitation, betrayal, oppression and injustice. Politicians repressed, oppressed and exploited the poor and the downtrodden in the past and now. There is no end to oppression and exploitation. The oppressed are constantly oppressed and will be forever in the society. Nobody actually thinks of them. They don't have the conviction to step up in life. They are not standing against the injustice. The main objective of the playwright is to make the readers aware of the exploitation, injustice, and oppression commonly practised in society.

History repeats itself. The past comes to the present. Time changes, the environment changes, and the characters get changed, but the suffering never ends. We can't think of a classless society in real life. The poor and the rich can't stand together in the same plane. While the hegemonic group enjoys all of society's facilities, the subdued group needs to be improved. It's an ever-lasting process—the play's powerful presentation of contemporary life links with the past. In epic format (episodic), different backgrounds are interconnected, and the songs are technically brought in to move from one to the next phase of unfolding facts and link the public sentiments well. There is no need for special characters in a dialogue-based play. Therefore, from that point of view, changing the characters is well-enshrined in the play.

This play is indeed successful and socially realistic. It will undoubtedly draw the attention of the readers with human sensitivity and lovers of drama.

Professor Niladri Bhusan Harichandan

Translator's View

The multi-coloured society has been subtly complex and structured beautifully since time immemorial. It gets handed down from generation to generation, relegating its dark and grim reality to the background. Beneath its social mosaic lies lurked the craftsmanship of the poor and the wretched, the voiceless and disadvantaged class of the society. Society ridicules their labour. But the world is yet to pay heed to their works they actually shoulder. The social hierarchy completely engulfs them and ignores their rights. They are deprived of their natural rights because they are weak financially. It is generally observed that the persons who hoard themselves with wealth, money and power are respected most. Money symbolizes the power that, in turn, gives rise to hierarchy. The people of all classes, directly or indirectly, are interpellated to this age-old system to show the rest of the world that they are disciplined community members. Everybody tends to shed light upon the brighter side or the rosy picture of society. The people have no courage to reflect upon the opposite side of the reality in which we are already suspended.

The playwright Narayan Sahoo brilliantly knocks on society's door to glance over the agonies and suffering the dominated class is experiencing daily through his *O Saba Sesha Loka*. I have translated this masterpiece from Odia into English as *And the Wretched*. Here, he focuses on how people experiencing poverty suffer unendingly and their voice is unheard diachronically. Moving across the axes of Time and Space, the picture remains almost the same, though the illustrations he has stated are of this Indian Peninsula. The powerless and the voiceless raise their voices against the powerful and dominant classes for approving their natural rights. The writer advocates the mantra (dictum), as prescribed in the dialogue of Great Man, can be simplified that nothing is possible through negotiation so far. The alternative to this is revolution, the means of ascertaining one's rights and individuality. He painstakingly cites Ekalavya's case from *the Mahabharat*, the historical case of the Sun Temple of Odisha and the contemporary society wherein we are all the subjects successfully. He has undoubtedly justified the title of his play. Let's look at the vignettes he has snapped in his creative oeuvre for the wider readership.

The first case is of the conspiracy Guru Drona had chalked out in India's well-celebrated mythology. Everyone is aware of the anecdote. As stated in the Mahabharat, Guru Drona has taught his disciples, both Kauravs and Pandavs. One day, following the decree of Guru Dronacharya, Duryodhan and his brothers moved into the woods searching for a rhino that urgently needed to be sacrificed to liberate the soul of Guru Krupacharya, who died earlier. None of them did trace any rhino in the forest and came across the wife of Jara Sabar (Ekalavya) and attempted to rape her. Because of her cry in distress, Ekalavya reached there and saved her from their evil intention. He shot the weapons, and all the Kauravs lost their sense for long. Guru and his disciple Arjun knew all this and requested Ekalavya to release them, as it was associated with his prestige. He innocently confessed,

"You are my Guru." I learnt this from you indirectly. I visited Varunabanta to learn this art of archery from you, but I have been denied for my caste. Ekalavya was second to none in archery at that time. All of them were given their life back, and as the *Guru-Dakshina* Ekalavya sacrificed the thumb of his right hand. Here the attention we should pay to the plight of the wretched, an innocent guy hailing from tribes suffered in three different ways: denial of education from Guru Dronacharya, the attempt to rape his wife, and the source of his livelihood, the thumb of his right hand. He suffered ceaselessly, and nobody looked at him.

The second issue concerns the construction of the Sun Temple of Odisha. When King Narasingh Dev decreed the establishment of a monumental work, the famous story, as accepted widely, says that twelve hundred sculptors were engaged in the job for twelve years to complete this work. The final touch toward the top of the temple is yet to be done. Then, there was an order for the sculptors to finish the temple within a week. Otherwise, they will be beheaded. Having heard this, all of them were in jeopardy. Then, the twelve-year-old son of principal sculptor Vishu Maharana reached there and completed the work and thereafter, plunged into the sea (the Bay of Bengal) to save the lives of the people of his community. Here again, the poor workers suffered a lot. Their misery is unspeakable. The sculptor couldn't visit their families and relatives when they wanted. Some of them died of hunger and starvation. Vishu Maharana lost his son publicly. Ultimately, the temple was built up as 'one of the seven wonders of the world', and the King became famous worldwide. The credit goes to the King, but what about the wretched community's feelings?

Through the third incident, the playwright draws our attention to the contemporary social life in which we are all participants. Before the elections, the people who want to contest visit the poor and distressed frequently as if they were blood-related to them, with many promises prescribed in the political manifesto. Once elected, they forget the people and do nothing for their betterment. The society gets polluted with the syndromes of exploitation, oppression, murder, anarchy, vandalism, deceitfulness, bloodshed, terror and menace. The ordinary people, especially the wretched, suffer chronically untold problems. The hegemonic group in power brutally tortures the distressed throughout history.

There is no nexus between the poor and the rich. The rich become more affluent, and the poor become poorer. The suffering of the poor never ends. To regain the rights, they must be aware of and revolt against the society.

I have tried my best to keep the language as lucid as possible. While following the rules of equivalence and the rules of fidelity between the Odia language and the English language, I came across some natural shifts. The culture-specific terms of the source language texts are maintained as they are. Some deictic expressions of the Odia language are marked in the target language while translating.

I deeply revere Professor Narayan Sahoo for believing me to translate his text carefully. He is a renowned professor of Odia Literature, retired from Utkal University. I convey my gratitude to Dr. Pradosh Kumar Swain, Assistant Professor, Department of Odia Language and Literature, Central University of Odisha, for helping me select this text for the stuff of my work.

I convey my heartfelt gratitude to Sri Satya Pattanaik, the director of Black Eagle Books, USA and Sri Ashok Parida of the publishing house for their kind consent to publish the texts in time.

Sanjeet Kumar Das

CONTENTS

Scene I
Scene-II
Scene-III
Scene-IV
Scene-V
Scene-VI
Scene-VII
Scene-VIII
Last Scene

About the Play *And the Wretched*

Dramatic Personae:

Great Man
Last Man
Front Man
Side Man
Middle Man
Own Man
Wretched Man
Other Man
Woman

[The play was staged by different Play Institutes of the state, at Department of Education and Youth Welfare, Odisha University of Agriculture and Technology, Utkal Sangeet Natak College, Premier Club, Shastriji Club Artist and Play Institute.]

The play *And the Wretched* was staged at Rabindra Mandap on 04.08.2011 (Thursday) on behalf of the Cultural Council of Odisha Secretariat. Mr Santosh Mohanty directed the play, and the co-director was Dhaneswar Sahoo. The Radio Play of this was 'The Last Step' (*Seshapahacha*), well-appreciated at the All India Level. This play has retained its pride while translated into English and Hindi. The play is well-recognized and translated from Odia into different regional languages and broadcast from other All India Radio stations in India.

SCENE-I

[The Map of India is displayed on the white screen in the stage light. In the central part of the Map is installed the Indian National Flag.

The steps are kept one above another and elongated from the lower part of the Map or Background Screen. The first step from the top is occupied by the Great Man, who meditates in Lord Avalokiteswara's position (i.e., the sleeping posture of Lord Buddha in which He has raised his hands to bless the devotees). On one side of the last step from the top or the first step from the button is the wretched, whose hands and legs are shackled.

On both sides of the three steps are placed some characters in different positions such as the 'Front Man' is in the style of taking liquor, the 'Own Man' in the style of murdering, 'Side Man' in the style of disrobing someone, and the 'Middle Man' in the style of whipping somebody. At a small distance from them the 'Last Man' is marching ahead holding the National Flag of India in his hands. The dim light of the stage slowly gets flooded. In the full-lit stage, the 'Last Man' sings the National Anthem of India. In the parade style, he is marching ahead. Because of his song, there are innumerable solid vibrations in the Great Man's body. The eyes of the older man get opened. The 'Great Man' comes down the steps with a strange euphoria.

The 'Last Man' looks at the 'Great Man' suddenly.

He stops there. He stops singing. Then the 'Great Man' runs to the 'Last Man'.]

Great Man	: Why do you stop?
Last Man	: (Silent)
Great Man	: Sing…sing once more.
Last Man	: (Silent)
Great Man	: Why do you stop abruptly? Sing it wholeheartedly. My song…the song of my race…
Last Man	: (Smiling)
Great Man	: I am disturbed by your smile.
Last Man	: (In the smile, there is scorn.)
Great Man	: Stop,…stop this smile.
Last Man	: Why will I stop smiling?
Great Man	: Who are you? Why are you smiling like this?
Lat Man	: I am 'Last Man'.
Great Man	: Don't you recognize me? I am 'Great Man'.
Last Man	: Oh, then you are that Great Man! (Ridiculing with contempt)
Great Man	: You have all forgotten me. But I have always remembered my 'Golden Bharat' and will remember her. For her freedom, I have tolerated and suffered a lot smilingly.
Last Man	: (Again smiling)
Great Man	: Last Man, you are again smiling.

Last Man	:	(He becomes serious.)
Great Man	:	Your smile is full of scorn.
Last Man	:	Perhaps, you are right.
Great Man	:	But,…why?
Last Man	:	You have suffered for the freedom of the country only. But, you have never experienced the agonies that come after our country's Independence. How dangerous that suffering is!
Great Man	:	In this auspicious day…
Last Man	:	(Looking at the face of Great Man)
Great Man	:	How will you know the love I have for my land, Last Man? How will you judge my love for the country? In this land are hidden so many unforgettable stories and sagas of suffering that I had gone through.
Last Man	:	It has been too late.
Great Man	:	What do you say?
Last Man	:	This speech is the last one.
Great Man	:	No, Last man…
Last man	:	Last Man is living only to die. To live for him is to suffer.
Great Man	:	Last Man!
Last Man	:	Both life and death are equal to that man whose life is almost dull, dead and dry; whose livelihood is to struggle (merchandise) daily.

Great Man	: But, what do I hear this day? I had never imagined the conditions of the people like you would be so disastrous as it is now, in my 'Dream India'.
Last Man	: You have made us independent only, but the agonies and sufferings of the people in life are more than that of British India (Colonial India).
Great Man	: Last Man!
Last Man	: Every individual of Bharat (India) is inflicted with the germ of waywardness/wilfulness at every hair pore of the body. Into the *Yajnavedi* (altar) of self-interest are thrown the individuals alive.

[From the background is heard the song. Both of them stand unmoved till the music completes.]

"O Brother, if one's self-interest is the charioteer, Will the race-*Nandigosh* move?

If the mouth of a horse is tied with a bag full of grains, Will the horse pull the chariot?"

Great Man	: What are you saying, Last Man?
Last Man	: You are responsible for this misfortune of India.
Great Man	: Me! Am I responsible?
Last Man	: Yes, you are!
Great Man	: Have I been wrong in rendering new life to India?
Last Man	: What have you done right?

Great Man	: Last Man!
Last Man	: Today, the country's oppression is in no way less than the harassment of the foreigner. It has reached its peak. For whom?
Great Man	: Am I responsible for this?
Last Man	: Yes, You! Of course, it would have been better that day.
Great Man	: No, Last Man, no! Don't distort my dream of ages so rudely.
Last Man	: Dream, again in you! (Smilingly)
Great Man	: Last Man, don't restrict the value of Independence like this. I have experienced the torture of Foreigners smiling.
Last Man	: There was no life in that oppression!
Great Man	: Last Man! You are denying my sacrifice for the freedom of India.
Last Man	: Yes! (With long breath) Your maxim and epigrams of freedom are confined to only a handful of few self-centric people. That's a terror for the oppressed and the poor who live from hand to mouth.
Great Man	: Last Man!
Last Man	: You have come. See your most loved the wretched ones. Your love for them never ends. [He hints at the subaltern. Great Man looks at the miserable with full of tears in his eyes. He has released him from the shackles. The wretched become active.]

Great Man : Wretched Man! Why are you here in this state? What do I see?

Wretched Man: You gave me new life…you brought me from darkness to light. But in your golden India, my power was very limited.

Great Man : No…!

Wretched Man: I don't have the right to live on this land.

Great Man : Wretched Man!

Wretched Man: Wretched Man is oppressed daily and will be crushed forever. The stored agony is as if solely written in his life! For him, the whole world is very selfish.

Great Man : (Being heartbroken) I have freed the nation from the British Raj (Rule) for you only.

Last Man : But, the wretched man is deprived of that. The Sun of Independence is, as if, prohibited for him.

Great Man : In my preparation, was there any weakness somewhere? Having suffered a lot, I-

Last Man : The people in whose name, for whom, and by whom the country became independent stayed all behind the screen forever.

Great Man : O Indians! Did I expect all this from you? (Looking at the audience)

Last Man : The hopes and aspirations of the wretched are tangled in the circular array of exploitation, oppression, scarcity and poverty. Independence is associated with the hegemonic group. At the hints of the

	privileged, Independence is auctioned at a meager price.
Great Man	: All these happened, but you had been the silent spectators. Why?
Wretched Man:	I opposed.
Last Man	: All oppositions were fruitless.
Wretched Man:	I also threatened agitation and revolted.
Last Man	: The revolution surrendered before the hegemonic or dominant power.
Wretched Man:	I had been deprived of my rights.
Last Man	: This is the privileged dominant group.
	[He points at the Front Man, Side Man, Own Man, and Middle Man. Great Man looks at them once. He is outraged. His body shivers with anger and contempt.]
Great Man	: In your hands…yes, have I handed over 'Country's Independence' that day for this? Answer me…answer my question. Why are you silent? (Taking a turn towards the audience) All my dreams and all possibilities are useless today. I wanted a New India in the documents signed for freedom, where we are all one irrespective of caste, creed and colour, and the sons of one mother. (He is heartbroken. He is about to cry because of grief and anguish in his heart, but he controls himself.) What happened? You all have broken into pieces what I have nurtured in my hands!

Last Man	: Nothing lies here except the repetition of history.
Great Man	: But I wanted a 'Rama Rajya' (An ideal government).
Last Man	: Rama Rajya was not entirely set free from sins and turbidity.
Great Man	: Last Man!
Wretched Man	: There was not a place for him too. Ramachandra was only a king.
Last Man	: What sin Shambuk had committed? For what had he been sentenced to death? The fault was this that-
Wretched Man	: He didn't wear the sacred thread.
Last Man	: He didn't bless King Ramachandra, raising his hands.
Wretched Man	: He was not grouped in the community.
Last Man	: He was not licking the feet of those with spiritual knowledge.
Wretched Man	: And he was an untouchable,...*Sudra* (the fourth caste of the Indian caste system).
Last Man	: The wretched have never experienced their natural rights for ages. Their agony and distress increase in the community. Everybody steps up higher and higher, smothering them. They are crushed. Then, what have they received? Only obsession... obsession...obsession, nothing else.
Wretched Man	: I had no hope for power, honour and wealth. I didn't expect all this. I wanted to

	settle somewhere peacefully in this land. I didn't care for leading my life, being half-fed or in starvation. I was searching for a small hut…a little peace… a straightforward life…yes, simple life…
Last Man	: That was also banned for him.
Great Man	: Last Man!
Last Man	: In the prohibited area, he was an exiled prisoner. To live life for him was a cry of distress. In their fate are only written the sorrows and sufferings.
Great Man	: Now I am stirred inside. (Being disturbed)
Last Man	: This is the beginning. Have patience…
Great Man	: Last Man!
Last Man	: Every page of history is coloured today with the hot tears of the Wretched Man. Neither have they received any justice nor will they receive it in future.
Great Man	: No, Last Man! He has the right to live on this soil. Time will decide the best. You have to wait with patience till that moment.
Last Man	: Forbearance! How many days? For whom?
Wretched Man	: Every page of my life is stored with innumerable promises.
Last Man	: All the promises are today getting deceived and shattered. All forbearance comes to an end to the cry of distress of the famine.
Great Man	: No, Last Man, I will undoubtedly come up with a solution.

Last Man : What kind of solution will you bring? You can't do anything for them. They have been wounded for Ages, and will also be wounded forever.

(Light off)

[Other Man comes to the stage-front and starts singing.]

Other Man : O people! Be alert, and listen to what I say,

I will describe what had happened in past.

O learned men, let's visit the city of Hastina,

Roaming, we will behold all the vignettes of India.

There was a family of one King in Hastina City,

World-famous was it as the Soma Dynasty.

The city was known for the brave Guru Drona,

Who was teaching both Kuru-Pandav earnestly?

(Light Off)

SCENE-II

[After the stage light, it's observed that Guru Dronacharya trains his disciples the archery. Front Man acts as Guru Dronacharya, and in the position of disciples are Side Man, Own Man and Middle Man. Side Man and Own Man are setting the arrows to the bow string. Looking downward, the Middle Man uses the point of the arrow upward. Front Man looks at the sky. When the arrow is shot, it reaches the goal.]

Front Man : Bravo!…Bravo! The warrior Partha! I know it very well; you are the only one to point at the goal.

Middle Man : You are the cause of my success, Gurudev. With your blessing, this poor guy can make any impossible thing possible.

Front Man : Great Arjun! Guru Drona's blessing is always with you and will be forever.

Middle Man : (Bowing his head down, he seeks blessings.)

Front Man : My meditation and perseverance are fulfilled after a long time. Because of my foresight, you, Dhanjaya, will be invincible.

Middle Man : *"gurubrahmaa, guruvishnu, gurudev maheswara, guru saksaata parambrahma, tasmai shri gurave namah."*

(Bowing his head down, he seeks blessing.)

Front Man : Brave Arjun!

Middle Man : Gurudev!

Front Man : The success you achieved now is the result of the work of your earlier life. Your talent will remain undimmed in the world until the Sun and the moon are in the sky. Time will never dishonour your talent.

Middle Man : The creation will never disrespect the Creator, the Almighty.

Front Man : My boy! That Time has already come. Your training has come to an end. The new Sun is going to shine on the eastern horizon.

Middle Man : All the wishes of the Creator will be fulfilled. The creation will live for ages in the unending blessing of the Creator.

Front Man : Brave Dhananjaya! Only you can shape my perseverance and colour my dream…the dreams of so many days.

Middle Man : Blessings of Guru make my path easy and accessible. At the hints of the Creator, the creation can move ahead… move ahead to a distance. Heavy rainfall, the forest full of wild creatures, perilous road…all these will be insignificant to him.

Front Man : I have that firm conviction, mighty Phalguni!

Middle Man : Having received the blessings of Guru, Partha will be victorious. Blood, flesh, bone marrow and every part of him will be pronounced with only one voice:
'Om guruve namah om guruve namah.'

Front Man	:	Warrior Arjun! That day will be the day of the final test of the guru-shishya relationship, the day Guru Drona will be defeated in the hands of his disciple Arjun in learning and intelligence.
Middle Man	:	Gurudev!
Front Man	:	Don't lose your heart, my child! That's the rule of an Aryan. My hand-made pot will serve rice for me. What else can be happier than this? Guru Drona's life will be blessed and virtuous that day, This idea of guru-tradition will be for ages; the learning of Guru Drona's knowledge.
Middle Man	:	Can this pauper fulfill your great hopes, Gurudev?
Front Man	:	I have explored the volcano. One day, there will be a volcanic eruption. That day, the world will know, Drona's vow will be fruitful, Guru's judgment is excellent, Acharya's fire is burning bright.
Middle Man	:	Gurudev!
Front Man	:	That day will be the last day of my test, My forbearance will come to an end, The warrior Dhananjaya will be of extra-ordinary power, of ever-burning talent in this world.

Middle Man : Gurudev, there is doubt in my mind.

Front Man : No, my child! Don't fear.
March ahead on the road,
Goal is not far away,
You will certainly achieve success.

Middle Man : But…

Front Man : Make yourself stronger,
Work hard to petrify your body,
Make your heart as strong as thunderbolt,
Let your legs be strong,
Go ahead without any fear,
Victory will be yours publicly.

Middle Man : Partha needs your blessing,
Placing Guru Drona's idol in heart,
Partha will create *Sandhi-Sartta-Vigraha*.

Front Man : Warrior Partha!
I want that only.
Drona will always be right.
The dream will come true that day.

Middle Man : Gurudev (Bowing down his head.)

Front Man : Don't think of the result,
However, hard and detrimental the case may be,
Let the world speak of you wrong,
Still, your aim is to reach the goal.

Middle Man : Touching your feet, I now promise,

              However, that may be heart-rending,

              Partha will never be away from the goal.

Front Man : Thank you, Arjun,

              For this only,

              Since time immemorial, I am waiting,

              River gets mingled with the sea,

              I will sleep peacefully now.

Middle Man : Till the time the soul lies in the body,

              Partha won't make any wrong use of knowledge,

              and Guru Drona's honour.

Front Man : *Sadhu…Sadhu…Sadhu!* (Good!)

Middle Man : *Satya…Satya…Satya,* Gurudev! I promise before you,

              The great wealth I have received from you will never be destroyed.

Front Man : Another truth you shouldn't forget,

              To live depriving others of something is not a sin;

              To concentrate on self-defense at the cost of others is not a crime.

Middle Man : Gurudev's blessing is only Partha's desire.

              [Drona meditates, and the light gets dimmed. After sometimes Drona invites.]

Front Man : My dear students !

All	: Gurudev! (They are all coming forward.)
Front Man	: Tomorrow Krupa's obsequies.
	Begetting Ashwatthama, he left the world forever.
All	: Gurudev!
Front Man	: The sight of that day, now before me dances.
	Krupa hoped a lot,
	But, the whole world obstructs him,
	Before seeing his son's birth,
	He breathed his last.
All	: Gurudev! What's order to us?
Front Man	: Everything is His plan and play,
	Human beings are only a ball.
	What's inevitable will happen one day.
	For Krupi's obsequies, there is the need of a rhinoceros,
	My dear students! Move into the dense forest immediately.
All	: Gurudev's order is certainly followed.

[With Gurudev's order, Side Man and Own Man enter the forest. In the deep woods, they have reached a common spot while searching for the rhinoceros from different directions. By that time all of them are tired.]

Side Man	: The rhinoceros is not visible at all.
Own Man	: This forest is bizarre!

[As if from the forest, the rhinoceroses were withdrawn. We are exhausted!]

Side Man	: Then, what's our duty now? Will we return?
Own Man	: *Kshetriya* will lose its fame forever!
Side Man	: This will be disrespect to our Guru.
Own Man	: At least, for one more attempt we should take.
Side Man	: If we don't see any rhinos?
Own Man	: The Kuru Dynasty's blood is not loose and slack.
Side Man	: Of course, the body needs rest.
Own Man	: The germ of tiredness in *Kaurav*'s blood!

[He laughs loudly.]

Side Man	: Be vigilant, the brave man! Time is inauspicious and unfavourable. The hope of getting rhinos weakens..
Own Man	: Don't dishearten yourself, brother!

At a distance is seen the dense forest,

Our hope may be fulfilled there.

Side Man	: You will hint at me in case of any danger!
Own Man	: Danger! (Half-smiling)

I am not frightened.

In Kuru Dynasty's blood can be a whirlpool,

But, no tremor will be observed.

(The stage is lit after a short break.)

Other Man : I am describing what happened thereafter,...

The disciples of the Gurukula (Ashram) were roaming helter-skelter in the deep forest. There was no trace of rhinos in the woods, full of wild creatures. But, their eyes were fixed on a woman bathing in the waterfall flowing down the mountains.

[Other man leaves. Infatuated Own Man comes to the woman for sex.]

Own Man : What a pleasing fountain inside the deep forest! Our thirst will surely be fulfilled.

(The Woman becomes bashful and conscious of their presence.)

Own Man : Don't fear!

Woman : (She looks frightened.)

Own Man : I am from the *Gurukula* and born into a King's family. Fulfill my thirst by offering water.

Woman : Grown up in the Royal blood, you are so uncultured and uncivilized!

Own Man : *Sundari* (Damsel), you don't know! The person who wants food will rarely distinguish between good and bad or between what's just and what's unjust.

Woman : You are so mean. Try to know my husband who is very formidable and unassailable. You will be shot dead with his arrows.

Own Man : Hi, Pretty Woman! Please come to me.

I am impatient now,

Because of thirst,

I don't have fear for life if it gets lost for you.

Woman	:	Remember that another's wife is a mother-figure.
Own Man	:	(Laughing) Hah…hah…why do you articulate the word 'mother' without any cause?
		(Laughing, he comes to her. The Woman screams.)
Woman	:	Swami…i…i… (She cries for help from his husband.)
		[There is a vibration in the forest. Wretched Man becomes conscious of his wife's voice and dashes. Then he observes Own Man doing some mischief.]
Wretched Man:		O…Scoundrel…your stupidity and misbehavior,
		Quit this place as quick as possible,
		Otherwise, I will send you *Yamaalaya*. (I will kill you.)
Own Man	:	(Laughing) hah…hah…Being a *sabar* (one hailing from a tribe), you are so arrogant.
Wretched Man:		Why are you inviting death intentionally?
Own Man	:	No need to listen to your useless words,
		If you have hope for life,
		Hand over this damsel to me.
Wretched Man:		Stupid! Don't be attracted toward the rose,
		Looking at its colour,
		The prickles behind it are more dangerous.

Own Man : An insect in the forest can be so arrogant! I can send you *Yamaalaya* (Abode of *Yama Raj*) immediately if I want.

Wretched Man: I am sure, you will die. If you love your life, surrender before the Woman to pardon you.

Own Man : Taking birth in *Kshetriya*-caste, will I request for life? Stupid, the blood of the King of Hastina is not so loose and slack.

Wretched Man: Being a *Kshetriya*, how can you be so mean? *Dhik* (a word denoting contempt) to your caste! *Dhik* to your dynasty! *Dhik*, to your learning!

Own Man : O Shameless *Sabar* (a guy of a tribe)! Hand over to me the Woman at once. Otherwise,...

Wretched Man: O mean fellow! Now take the reward of your pride and haughtiness.

[Wretched Man and Own Man are in a strong faceoff and close fight. Own Man gets defeated and falls. There is Own Man's cry for help. Woman and Wretched Man leave the place.]

[Out of fear, Side Man loiters here and there in the forest. After roaming for some time, he has explored Own Man gets wounded.]

Side Man : 'Brother'...'Brother'! You don't hint me before danger.

[The Side Man is disturbed. He is unable to decide what to do next.]

How has it happened? No...impossible. It's impossible.

[Out of pride of being the blood of the Royal

Dynasty, he searches for the hunter for a while and does not see anyone.]

Side Man : Where do you hide, the mean fellow? Come to the front and I don't believe in deceitful fights. Knowingly, you have raised a battle with a lion's cubs. You are really a mean person.

[At the cry of Side Man, wretched Man reaches there.]

Wretched Man: O, you are also a part of that blood race.

Side Man : Stupid! You don't know whom you have killed. A tribal guy, you are so proud. If I want, you can be sent to heaven within no time.

Wretched Man: Time will decide who loves most, heaven or hell.

Side Man : You are unaware of the Royal blood! That's why you are so proud today.

Wretched Man: If you love to live, invoke your God, the Almighty. Please leave me alone, Stupid!

Side Man : Stupid! To whom are you advising? I am the pride of Kuru-dynasty…will I learn from you?

Wretched Man: For your nature, you seem to be of different origin.

Side Man : O mean fellow! Receive now the suitable reward for your arrogance.

Wretched Man: When death is in someone's fate, how can he avoid it?

Side Man : I am not here to hear the couplets of morality,

    I don't have the patience to spend my energy.

Wretched Man: A stupid fellow! ... an arrogant man!

    Take your reward now.

    [Both of them fight severely. Side Man falls down wounded. Wretched Man quits the spot confidently.]

Side Man : Ah...(a cry of distress) 'Gurudev'...

Wretched Man: Hah...hah...hah... (Leave)

    [The light gets slightly dimmed. Front Man, while meditating, gets disturbed. Beside him is the Middle man.]

Front Man : What's this? (Being surprised)...How can it be possible?

Middle Man : Gurudev! You are disturbed! Order me how this servant can help you? Please order me.

Front Man : There is an unnatural vibration within me.

Middle Man : This is perhaps the *psychological fear*.

Front Man : No, warrior, no...!

Middle Man : Then?

Front Man : There is still suspicion in my mind,

    Perhaps, they are in danger.

Middle Man : Kuru-king Duryodhan,

    Accompanied by the best warrior Duhshasan,

	And with them are so many warriors of the Kuru dynasty.
	Will they face any danger?
	Impossible! Impossible!
Front Man	: Still, I doubt,
	Why is there a vibration in the earth?
	By nature, the princes of the Kuru dynasty are so mean.
Middle Man	: Gurudev!
Front Man	: Yes, my child!
Middle Man	: Then, what's the way?
Front Man	: There is no other way except inquiry.
Middle Man	: You take rest, please.
	I enquire about them.
Front Man	: Both of us will enquire about them at once,
	[Front Man and Middle Man get into the forest and move ahead. They are on the way, full of thorns.]
Middle Man	: Gurudev! We are unable to trace them.
Front Man	: My child! Upon the nearby mountain-
	[Middle Man moves up the mountain for inquiry. After searching for a while, having seen the unconscious bodies of two brothers, he starts shouting 'Gurudev'!]
Front Man	: Partha!
Middle Man	: They are all here, fallen on the ground.

[Front Man and Middle reach the spot.]

Front Man : But, how has it been possible?

Middle Man : There must be a strong archer hiding in this forest.

Front Man : I doubt so. That potent bowman or archer has mastered *Purshuram Vidya* (Knowledge). But, this I have not taught anybody except you.

Middle Man : Then I make an inquiry of this, Gurudev!

Front Man : Yes, brave man! Go ahead!

[While the Middle Man searches atop the mountain, the Front Man walks agitatedly. Having seen a civilized man in his territory, Wretched Man becomes alert.]

Wretched Man: O...you are also of that vile blood-

Middle Man : To my brothers...!

Wretched Man: You are undoubtedly unhappy.

I will also send you *Yamaalaya*. You can't escape from me.

[The forest land reverberates with the sound of battle and Front Man is disturbed.]

Front Man : What's this? Why is the earth vibrating? Perhaps...Partha is in danger.

Otherwise-

[While searching for Middle Man for a while, he meets both of them on the battlefield.]

Front Man : Stop...stop this battle.

	Dhananjaya! It's my order.
	[Nearing Wretched Man]
	What's your name, warrior? I have never seen this kind of battle in my life.
Wretched Man	: I was born into a tribal caste. My name is Ekalavya.
Front Man	: Ekalavya! Wherefrom have you learnt this? Who's your Guru (Teacher)?
Wretched Man	: My Guru is Acharya Drona.
Front Man	: Acharya Drona! (Surprised) Impossible!
Wretched Man	: Yes, I have learnt this education from Guru Dronacharya.
Front Man	: I am that Guru Drona.
	But I have never taught you.
Wretched Man	: Please pardon me, Gurudev!
	[Wretched Man prostrates before Gurudev.]
Front Man	: Get up, my child! Clear my doubts. How have you mastered this?
Wretched Man	: With lots of hope that day, I moved to Barunabanta. But Duryodhan, like the Kauravs, had deprived me of education from you. Humiliated I was, and I returned from Barunabanta, I made and established a statue of Drona in clay on the hilltop. I surrendered myself before him in thoughts, words, and deeds. What you teach your disciples was

	closely observed by me, though I was at a distance of *dwadasha yojana* (i.e., approximately 153 kilometers) away from you.
Front Man	: Good!...good! Ekalavya! My children are senseless. They are all the Kuru-dynasty princes and King Dhrutarastra's children.
Wretched Man:	Ekalavya's birth is fruitful, Gurudev!
Front Man	: I am very much pleased with your perseverance and training, Ekalavya! My request to you is to make all the dead-like disciples alive. Guru Drona's respect is dependent upon them.
Wretched Man	: It's not a request, but the order...Om gurave namah...(Thrice) [When the arrows of disillusionment are released, Side Man and Own Man get up and they are shocked to see others there.]
Front Man	: Well done...well done, Ekalavya! Your learning is unparalleled!
Side Man	: Gurudev! What mistake have the Kauravs made? For what have they faced such a disaster?
Own Man	: Is there any want in Hastinapur? For what have you been so revengeful to us?
Front Man	: Try to understand, my child!

Side Man	: What's left to understand? What we learn from Guru Drona is failed before a tribal guy.
Own Man	: Useless our learning! *Dhik* Guru Drona! It's better not to return Barunabanta with this defamed life.
Side Man	: Why have you deceived us?
Front Man	: Guru Drona is indebted to the Kaurav dynasty until he leaves the world. He never disrespects anybody of the dynasty. At least once, try to understand me, my child!
Side Man	: What else is left? Caste! …Race!… Respect! In the hands of uncivilized tribal guy, we are… It's better to embrace 'Death' than this.
Front Man	: Try to understand once, my child! He is the best warrior Ekalavya. You can be reminded of the person whom you insulted and returned from Barunabanta. [Having heard from Front Man, both are ashamed of and bowed down before him.]
Front Man	: My child, Ekalavya! Stay happily in the forest! We return to Barunabanta.

Wretched Man	: I have recognized you very late. It will be an injustice if you don't receive any *guru-dakshina* (honorarium paid to a teacher) from me. Be merciful to me to receive this…please, Gurudev!
Front Man	: Ekalavya! (Agitated)
Wretched Man	: Order me, please, Gurudev! If you want, I can be beheaded at your feet. Order me without any hesitation.

[Front Man looks at both Own Man and Side Man. They have withdrawn their faces.]

Front Man	: Ekalavya! (Lines of cunning and guile in the face)
Wretched Man	: Be determined to order me, please, Gurudev! (He bows down at Guru's feet.)
Front Man	: Ekalavya! You have to promise!
Wretched Man	: Gurudev! Is there any doubt, as I hail from a lower caste?

"gurubrahma guru Vishnu gurudeva Maheshwar! Promise…promise…promise…"

Front Man	: My child! Guru Drona's heart is hard and cruel. It's more complicated than thunderbolt. It can always be solid and flaccid. Guru…that only Guru…
Wretched Man	: Please order me, Gurudev! Why are you trembling now? You can say without any doubt, Gurudev…

Front Man	: Ekalavya! I want the thumb of your right hand. That's only my *Dakshina*... (Ekalavya gets shocked.)
Wretched Man	: Let there be victory for Gurudev! Om gurave namah...om gurave namah... om gurave namah!
	[While surrendering his thumb, Guru Drona is full of tears. He utters few words with much difficulty.]
Front Man	: Ekalavya! I accept this. Upon this earth, you are only the true warrior.
	[All of them take leave. Wretched Man suffers. The Woman comes slowly to him. Wretched Man takes rest at Woman's lap. Light off.]

SCENE-III

[Everything remains unaltered. Last Man describes his past experiences page after page. Great Man listens to it attentively without any wink of an eye.]

Last Man	: How will you solve their problem?
Great Man	: Still, I am not weak. Have faith in me. I will do something for them.
Last Man	: What will you do? Who will listen to you?
Great Man	: I have made them independent. I have helped them smile. I have supplied food for them to have. They will undoubtedly listen to me.
Last Man	: Since that day, in this world, so many amendments have been made. What kind of amendment do you want? Man gets petrified, bearing sorrows and sufferings a lot. Who will listen to your life song? Who will bring new life by that? Will they pay any heed to your call or invitation?
Great Man	: The surroundings have made them convicted. But they are holy like the water of the river Ganga.

Last Man	: Had one got salvation after bathing in the river Ganga, the frogs would have been made holy first!
Great Man	: At least for the last time I can.
Last Man	: Striving hard a lot, they couldn't end themselves. All their endeavours were in vain at last.
Great Man	: Still, I say, they will listen to me.
Last Man	: If you invoke the lifeless entities a hundred times with prayers, they will never get up.
Great Man	: Can a son throw his old father, thinking of him as useless?
Last Man	: There may be streams in the river of love and affection, but that's of the perennial flow.
Great Man	: Last Man!
Last Man	: Not only have you reached old age, but all your hopes and expectations are clouded with dust. To clear that cobweb, you have to take another birth.
Great Man	: No, Last Man!
Last Man	: Then, you can say… What was the fault of Ekalavya? Why had he been deprived of his right to live? Answer, answer my question.
Great Man	: I had my dream of converting Hastina Kingdom into heaven.

Last Man	: Hastina was also oppressed by the brokers of a capitalistic society like Drona.
Great Man	: Last Man! Don't make fun of the word 'Guru'.
Last Man	: Ekalavya had a lot of hopes for his Guru Drona! But what had he received? Was it a suitable reward for his reverence for Guru? Drone was an embodied panegyric or eulogist of Monarchy.
Great Man	: He had no other option.
Last Man	: Cowards could have taken the suicidal attempts.
Great Man	: Last Man!
Last Man	: Only because of him is the history blamed. The teacher-student relationship is bitter.
Great Man	: Last Man!
Last Man	: To safeguard and preserve the Monarchy is to uproot the wretched and the downtrodden. Was it the need of that hour?
Great Man	: Last Man!
Last Man	: Because of Guru Drona's treachery, Ekalavyas are now wounded and bruised at different corners of the earth. Their cry of distress never ends.
Great Man	: All the hopes get dissolved like bubbles in water. I wanted *Ramarajya* (An ideal government), but what have I got?

Last Man	: There was also the wretched dreaming of death every moment. Justice was also a denial for them.
Great Man	: No, Last Man, No! Don't blame '*Ramarajya*'.
Last Man	: *Ramarajya*…! What crime had Shambuka committed? Why had Rama sentenced him to death? To be very frank, the rule of Ramachandra was not meant for the downtrodden. There were also the sufferings of daily workers and wage labourers. Ramachandra was a king, but a ball in the hands of *Brahmanical* Society and a toy only.
Great Man	: Last Man!
Last Man	: There is no need to realize all this. The agonies and issues of the wretched are and will be in the society. Their suffering never ends and won't end. What had he received in the Middle Age? [Light off]

Topic Scene

[Other Man enters the stage, when the stage is lit.]

Other Man : After all that had happened…

The intellectuals don't see the faults,

In the meanwhile, the story of one age is complete.

For ages are the sufferings of the downtrodden,

If we sit to describe, the story still needs to be completed.

Battles are always fought in this Indian land,

You know, one is sacrificed at the cost of the other.

Monarchy and Clan Systems are the forms of Government,

In every government lies a hidden principle.

Nobody pays attention to the objectives of commoners,

In the name of the King of the state, personal interest reigns.

This Time, Ladies and Gentlemen, are alert to what I say. It's not a false story.

It's based on reality. Let's start judging our history.

(*Dasakathia* performance Style)

O Intellectuals! Let's move to the holy place Chandrabhaga,

where Emperor Narasingh Dev had decreed for the Sun Temple.

Having given up food, sleep and sex,

Day and night engaged in the work are twelve hundred sculptors.

They have forgotten their homes and families,

Their goal was to build the Sun Temple.

On this earth, this monument will stand imperishable,

The world will say, "Let there be victory for Narasingh!"

Come…come…let's meet the poor and the downtrodden,

Though they are known as the sculptors, they are live skeletons.

SCENE-IV

[The image of Konark is set on the screen. After the stage is lit, Wretched Man and Middle Man are engaged in temple-building and join them the Side Man and Own Man. They are all twelve hundred sculptors. They have forgotten everything about their personal life after joining work. Last Man comes slowly. He makes an attempt to study the surroundings of the temple.]

Last Man : Can you hear me for a while?

[He calls everybody, but nobody listens to him. O, nobody is interested to hear me! What work are they engaged in? He reaches the Wretched Man. Can you hear me?]

Wretched Man : (He is working indifferently.)

Last Man : Can you hear me now?

Wretched Man : Are you asking me?

Last Man : No, I am asking the stones! (Jokingly)

Wretched Man : Yes, you can.

It will respond to you.

If you develop a relationship with it, it will also talk to you friendly.

Last Man : Oh! Working with the stones, they have also been petrified.

Wretched Man : What else, if it's not that!

Had we not been stones with stones, how would we have built such a great temple like Konark?

I have made the stones smile in this hand.

I have made the stones drop tears in this hand.

In this hand, in this hand!

I am building my dream Konark!

The Konark of the sculptor's life!

The Konark of Art and Architecture!

Last Man : Is a sculptor only the sculptor?

Does he not have life at all?

Wretched Man : I have spent sleepless nights.

I have forgotten my thirst and hunger,

for this Konark only.

The sculptor will surely die one day,

But his sculpture won't.

Till Konark lives on earth,

In its every statue will live the sculptor!

What else can a sculptor expect more than this?

Last Man : Oh Sculptor! Why are you forgetting that?

Are you also a human?

In your every artery flows–

	Hot blood of social life!
	You have a family,
	You have a society,
	You also have a different style of living!
Wretched Man	: Life…Family…Society…all these!
	Are all these of mine?
Last Man	: Wife…Daughter…Son…! Father…Mother…Brother…!
Wretched Man	: Have I all these? But…but,
	[The eyes of Wretched Man are full of tears.]
Last Man	: Say, "What have you done for them?"
Wretched Man	: I have never thought of them.
	I have also yet to get time to think of them.
	Because of the King's decree-
	"Konark will be unparalleled in art and sculpture in the world. The sculptural beauty of this Sun temple will stand conspicuous and intact forever. The fate of twelve hundred sculptors is dependent upon the temple's fate. If the construction work of the temple isn't complete in time, and any indiscipline is marked in the work, the life of all twelve hundred sculptors will be at risk."
	[The dialogue of the King will be read out by Front Man.]

Wretched Man	: That order was very detrimental…fearful…severe…!
	That order was the communiqué or bulletin for twelve hundred sculptors.
	For twelve years, I have been struggling only
	with the stones.
	My blood, flesh, bone marrow… everywhere
	Only one attraction
	If we have to live-
	We have to build up this Konark,
	world famous and celebrated.
Last Man	: King…! Order…! Temple…! Idols and statues…!
	There is also life outside all this?
	You have struggled for twelve years with the stones;
	But not with you!
	With body, but not with the soul!
Wretched Man	: What else would I do?
	[He suffers from pain.]
Last Man	: I had a lot to work on.
	But twelve hundred sculptors-
	You all remain effeminate and eunuch forever!

You have all lost your twelve years!

You have dishonoured the human race!

[Last Man blames them all.]

Wretched Man : No...no...no...!!! (Agitated)

Last Man : You are responsible for your wife's death!

You are responsible for your son's illness!

You are responsible for your daughter's adulthood!

You are responsible for destroying Vishwakarma's large family!

Yes, you, you...you...!!!

Wretched Man : Am I responsible for all this?

Last Man : Nobody else other than you!

You have blamed history!

You are responsible for the loss of time!

Wretched Man : I have only obeyed the Order of the King.

Have I made any mistake honouring the Monarchy?

Have I made any mistake making Konark world famous?

Have I made any mistake paying respect to my sculpture?

Have I made any mistake in making the art of my caste alive?

	Have I made any mistake in soaring high the national prestige to the international one?
Last Man	: Race can be united,
	Art can be modified, and
	Heritage can be respected.
	But, the whims of twelve hundred sculptors can't be forgiven!!
Wretched Man	: No...(A cry of distress)
Last Man	: You are lame...you are useless.
Wretched Man	: No...!
	(Wretched Man starts crying.)
Last Man	: Twelve hundred sculptors! You know,
	You have dishonoured one race,
	You have done injustice to its women and mothers,
	You have not executed your duties properly to the holy Mother Earth...!
	[Wretched Man holds his ears very tightly. Light off]

Topic Scene

[Other Man enters the stage after the light is on.]

Other Man : O Learned men!

What happens next is detailed here. The construction of The Sun Temple was built in time. But the twelve hundred sculptors were unhappy. An unknown fear disturbed them fully. Still, then, they eagerly waited for result. The inauguration of the Sun Temple neared. This day, King Narasingh Dev decided and announced to honour the art and sculpture of those twelve hundred sculptors, and for that, there was a preparation for a meeting. (Light off)

SCENE-V

[The stage is flooded with light. King Narasingh Dev is honouring the sculptors in the courtyard of the Sun Temple. A solemn proclamation is heard along with the sound of gongs and bells.]

Announcement : "The Sun Temple is completed after a long time. The dream of King Narasingh Dev is fulfilled now. For this, a great celebration is organized here. In that

	meeting, the King will honour all the twelve hundred sculptors for their best effort. So the sculptors are requested to receive their rewards with discipline."
Last Man	: Sri Sri Mahamahim Emperor Narasingh Dev enters the courtyard…the Gentlemen… Be alert…
	[Raja (Front Man) marches ahead slowly. He looks at the well-decorated surroundings of the courtyard once.]
Front Man	: Minister!
Side Man	: Emperor…!
Front Man	: In reality, Utkal is excellent today.
Own Man	: Please have your seat, My Lord!
	(Front Man sits.)
Front Man	: The hopes I had for many years get fulfilled. Utkal is made holy and sanctified, embracing the Sun God in her heart. I am fortunate enough to see this. Gurudev! I want, "Let worshiping the Sun God be spread worldwide." 'News'…
Side Man	: Emperor! There is a famine in the eastern parts of Odisha. Due to the least rainfall, everywhere is heard the cries of distress. Day by day, the villages are emptied of people.
Front Man	: The Sun Temple will be memorable and unique in the world history.

Own Man	: It is heard from the older people that they have never experienced a famine of this kind for the last hundred years.
Front Man	: In the chronicles of history the Emperor Narasingh Dev will live enshrined. Like the radiant, powerful Sun, his monument will be unsurpassable worldwide. Chief Minister…
Side man	: Emperor…
Front Man	: You read my 'Announcement Paper' for the twelve hundred sculptors.
Side Man	: Let the 'Announcement Paper' of the Emperor be read out publicly.
Own Man	: This is the 'Announcement Paper' of Mahamahim Emperor Narasingh Dev…!

It is for the knowledge of twelve hundred sculptors.

"I am very much pleased with the work of twelve hundred sculptors. As the construction work of the temple is over, I don't need their presence anymore. So they can return to their home freely and safely. Being satisfied with their works, I am honouring them the gifts…"

Side Man	: Now I request the twelve hundred sculptors; they calmly come and receive the royal gifts from Emperor Narasingh Dev.

Own Man	:	First, the Crown of Twelve Hundred Sculptors, Vishnu Maharana…
		[At a distance, Wretched Man, like a lunatic, is digging the sand in the courtyard of Sun Temple.]
Middle Man	:	Vishu Bhai…. E Vishu Bhai…
Wretched Man	:	(He is digging the sand indifferently.)
Middle Man	:	What are you digging?
Wretched Man	:	Here…here is hidden.
Middle Man	:	Who?
Wretched Man	:	(Silence please)
		Someone will hear…
		And will catch hold of him.
		He will never return to me…
		No, he won't…
Middle Man	:	Hey, why are you behaving like a mad person?
Wretched Man	:	Mad…! I am mad!
		Why am I mad?
		Yes, yes…You say why I am mad?
Middle Man	:	Hey, you are our leader, the crown gem of sculptors.
		The King has declared your name first.
Wretched Man	:	Does he call me? Why? What else will he take?
Middle Man	:	Hey, you will receive prizes…Prizes…

Wretched Man	:	Will I or Vishnu Maharana receive the prize?
Middle Man	:	Hey, Vishu Bhai! It's not the time of lunacy.
Wretched Man	:	You have all made me lunatic.

        This Vishu really wanted the identity of a father.

        But, all of you have made him a *Maharana* (a caste of sculptors), only *Maharana*, an artist, nothing else.

Middle Man	:	What are you doing here, Vishu Bhai?
Wretched Man	:	Is Vishu Maharana only a Vishwakarma…?

        Yes, yes,…He is only a *Maharana*…!

Own Man	:	'Vishu Maharana',… 'Vishu Maharana'
Middle Man	:	Hey, leave…

        (Pushing Vishu Maharana, he releases him before the King.)

Front Man	:	Vishu! Utkal is proud of having a sculptor like you.

        I am pleased with your artistry. I am honouring you for the long life of that sculptor. Please accept the same.

        (He receives the gift from the King.)

Wretched Man	:	This is Vishu's gift!

        This is the gift of twelve hundred sculptors.

	This is the reward for the life of a sculptor.
	This is the reward of twelve hundred years' perseverance...this gift.
	[Holding the gift, he sits unhappily. His eyes are full of tears.]
Own Man	: 'Bipada Maharana'... 'Bipada Maharana'...
	(Middle Man comes to the stage, receives the gift, and returns to his original position.)
	'Shankar Maharana'....' Shankar Maharana'
	(A woman is marching ahead.)
Side Man	: You?
Woman	: Yes, I!
Side Man	: O, you will receive on behalf of Shankar Maharana!
Woman	: No...
Side Man	: Then?
Woman	: I have come here to ask you the same question. Where is Shankar Maharana?
Side Man	: Where is Shankar Maharana? (To Own Man)
Front Man	: Chief Minister! Where is Shankar Maharana?
	(Side Man looks at Own Man. Own Man whispers to Side Man.)

Side Man	: My Lord! Shankar Maharana left the world three years back.
Own Man	: While Shankar Maharana was working, he abruptly came across a huge rock and got crushed there and then
Front Man	: He gets martyred/self-immolated for art and sculpture. It will be recorded for ages.
Woman	: The Emperor listens to all and donates what they want. Can I return from this place empty-handed?
Front Man	: No…! Nobody will return empty-handed from the Royal Court of Narasingh Dev. Neither had it happened, nor will it happen.
	O Woman! You say what you want. Do you need wealth or something else?
Woman	: Please, return me my husband Shankar Maharana, My Lord! I don't know anything else.
Front Man	: (Silence)
Woman	: I want my husband, My Lord!
Front Man	: Nobody returns from the other world once he leaves this world permanently. However, Shankar has breathed his last for the people of the land (i.e., for his caste and race of Odias). You should be proud of that. You, you should receive the royal gift in favour of him.

Woman	: I kick that gift of honour, My Lord!
Front Man	: A stubborn lady…! (The King shouts.)
Woman	: I have yet to come here to receive your royal gift. I have come here to take my husband back. If you can, return me, my most loved one.
Front Man	: O woman! This is the court of Emperor Narasingh Dev. If he wants-(Trembling)
Woman	: What else will he want?
	What else has he left?
Front Man	: "Obstinate woman"…before whom are you speaking uselessly?
Woman	: O King! Have you ever thought of those who have been stones with stones?
	Have you ever thought of twelve hundred sculptors?
	Have you ever realized that there is also a world of a sculptor?
	Have you ever realized that he has also a life?
Front Man	: A mere woman's arrogance before Narasingh Dev! I will punish you rightly.
Woman	: What kind of punishment will you give?
	You have snatched away a husband from his wife,…
	You have snatched away a son from his mother,…

	You have exploited twelve hundred sculptors…
	You have ruined their families…
	You…you…you…! Can you return all that?
Front Man	: Nobody dares to question the King so far.
	Only the King can question,
	Not to the King. (He trembles in anger.)
	"Minister…"
Side Man	: My Lord!
Front Man	: Give the stubborn Woman her due to the actual governance of the Monarchy.
	[Side Man and Own Man start dragging Woman.]
Woman	: O King! I curse you-
	The temple you have built up and erected, ruining the peaceful families of twelve hundred sculptors, won't stay long.
	Your dreams will vanish in the streams of hot tears of the starved.
	History will pardon you,
	But Time won't.
Front Man	: Commander-in-Chief! Throw this arrogant lady into the darkness of the prison.

	For her vibrant pride, she can't see the sunlight anymore on the earth.
Own Man	: Ok, My Lord!

[Side Man drags Woman and throws. Front Man, Side Man and Own Man leave. Revolving there for a while, Woman reaches Wretched Man at last. The woman cries out of pain. Resting her head in his lap, Wretched Man speaks on continuously…]

Wretched Man	: This is what the reward for twelve hundred sculptors.
	This reward is for art and sculpture and the community/race of sculptors.
	This is the reward for the poor and the downtrodden…
	[Wretched Man starts crying. The stage is lit off.

SCENE-VI

[After the stage light, it is observed that Last Man speaks incessantly and Great Man listens to the whole history.]

Great Man : What am I hearing…?

Last Man : If you entered the battlefield of Kuru-Pandav!

At least once, you would see how far your dream India is.

Great Man : Last Man! I am a human being…I have a heart.

Last Man : No, you are a lifeless stone.

Your movement stopped many years ago.

You are forever static and immovable.

Great Man : Last Man…!

Last Man : We can't believe you anymore.

Great Man : No, Last Man…no…!

My hands and legs are shackled.

I am still breathing in and out.

Nobody can control it. I am free and independent.

Last Man	: Yes! …Independent! (Jokingly)
Great Man	: Do you mock me?
Last Man	: Can you answer my questions?
	What crime had the twelve hundred sculptors committed?
	Why had they been completely ruined?
	Why was their perseverance of twelve years looted at a meager price?
	Why was the backbone of the subaltern destroyed?
	Why was the peak time of their life plundered?
Great Man	: Oh, Stop it! Stop it, Last man!
Last Man	: Where were you that day? Where was your breathing in and out of the air?
	Say, answer me….where was your independence?
Great Man	: Last Man!
Last Man	: What was the fault of the sculptors of Tajmahal?
	Why had they been forced to commit suicide?
	Their fault was that they had built up the world-famous monument.
Great Man	: O, the people of India (in a sorrowful tone)!
	You have devastated the 'Independence'

that I achieved with my blood and tears.

What crime had I committed then?

With many hopes, I handed over to you my dreams of ages that day.

But what did you give me? What did you give?

Last Man : Shedding the tears, you will not earn anything.

Time is over. Your dream vanishes.

There is a whirlpool of anarchy in the peaceful India.

Here, only the poor and the distressed are living to die.

Great Man : O, My people of India!

Had I expected all this from you?

Last Man : You are disturbed by this!

Come, you will receive the reward for what you have gifted.

You will see your dream India, and her successors, how they blow your conch of independence,

That you earned with hard labour.

[The light gets dimmed on the stage.]

Relevant Scene

[Other Man comes to the stage.]

Other Man : I am describing you what happens next,

O Learned men, hear me attentively!

Of two ages, you saw the downtrodden suffer,

Nobody was there to save them all.

Many ages went on like this,

The modern man plans for the battle of science.

For personal interest, Man becomes a goat,

The disease of politics engulfs the world.

[Let's return to the modern man now. It was evening. There was a clamour of election surcharging the atmosphere. Considering the upcoming election, the political party leaders were doing a door-to-door campaign. That evening, what had happened is as follows…]

SCENE-VII

[It's evening. A particular scene regarding the preparation of the General Election is brought to the limelight. Someone knocks on the door. Middle Man is calling, accompanied by Front Man and Own Man.]

Middle Man	: Are you at home, Rama Pradhan? Pradhane...are you at home? Is there anybody or not?
Wretched Man	: (From inside the house) Who's there?
	[He opens the door and looks at them strangely.]
Middle Man	: Why do you look at us so strangely?
Wretched Man	: (Silent)
Middle Man	: Babu has come. Mahapatrababu.
Wretched Man	: Oh, Mahapatrababu. Namaskar, Sir!
	(To the Woman) Hey, come to see who has come.
Woman	: (Touching his feet, she conveys her regard.)
Front Man	: I won't leave your home unless I take food. O *Bhauja* (Sister-in-law)! (To Woman) can I be served or not?

Wretched Man	:	What can this pauper serve you? After all, you are rich-
Woman	:	(Pulling her veil) We are the people with low incomes. What can we offer?
Front Man	:	That can't be avoided. I am the son of this soil. I have come to my area. Will I return without food?
Wretched Man	:	What will this poor offer ... to you, the rich...?
Front Man	:	Pradhane, see, telling yourself poor again and again, makes me ashamed of. Hello, one brother, has come to another brother. Respect is not sought at the brother's house.
Wretched Man	:	We are poor,...the downtrodden...
Front Man	:	Who is poor...who is rich? The same blood flows in everybody... the blood of humanity.
Wretched Man	:	Where is Ramachandra, and where is Rama Pradhan?
Front Man	:	There should be no discrimination among us. Yes, Pradhane! I won't leave this place without having anything.
		[Woman and Last Man look at each other.]
Side Man	:	Then, why so late?
Own Man	:	Let's start our business!
Middle Man	:	Yes, Pradhane! Babu's symbol-

Side Man	:	Horse Symbol
Own Man	:	Big horse
Middle Man	:	The fastest animal in the earth-
Side Man	:	Horse
Own Man	:	Our horse…Babu's horse
Middle Man	:	Horse can run with the speed of wind.
Side Man	:	It can cross the earth, water and fire effortlessly.
Own Man	:	The most trusted animal of the gods-
Side Man	:	Horse…
Middle Man	:	Of the human beings, too.
Front Man	:	If you vote on 'Horse Symbol'-
Own Man	:	We will fly. Our country will also run.

[Woman and Wretched Man couldn't understand anything.]

Side Man	:	Progress can gallop speedily at every step.
Middle Man	:	You won't forget your dear known "horse".
Side Man	:	From the teenagers to the older men and women-
Own Man	:	Only shelter-
Middle Man	:	Horse.
Front Man	:	If I win in the election-
Side Man	:	I will change the thatched houses.
Own Man	:	I will build the tile-roof houses.

Middle Man	: I will remove poverty from the country.
Own Man	: I will exempt you from the water tax.
Side Man	: I will free you of land revenues.
Middle Man	: I will provide the older men and women with the pension system.
Side Man	: I will provide you with the Indira Avash Yojana. (The scheme for building house)
Own Man	: I will help you get *the Individual Household Latrines Scheme.*
Front Man	: Pradhane! You are very poor. Like you, so many people are in this country. They are struggling hard in their life. Nobody has paid any attention to them. But, if I win in the General election,…
Middle Man	: I will provide the landless people rice at two rupees per kilogram.
Side Man	: I will provide the employed pension.
Own Man	: Net Loan for the fisherman
Middle Man	: Loan of *Paala* (A sheet of jute cloth) for the fisherman
Side Man	: Buffalo Scheme
Own Man	: Cow Scheme
Side Man	: Sheep Scheme
Own Man	: Goat Scheme
Middle Man	: Poultry Scheme
Side Man	: Duck Scheme
Own Man	: Scheme for flood

Middle Man	: Scheme for Storm
Own Man	: Scheme for Bicycle
Side Man	: Scheme for Rickshaw
Own Man	: Scheme for Bullock-Cart
Middle Man	: Scheme for Seed
Side Man	: Scheme for Fertilizer
Middle Man	: Scheme for Manure
Middle Man	: Loan…Scheme…Scheme…Loan!
Front Man	: Nobody thinks of the country that gets degraded day by day. Corruption, vandalism, riots, and plundering are everywhere in the country. People experiencing poverty become poorer now and then. No one thinks of their development. But, if I win in the election-
Middle Man	: I will offer you the sun of progress in the palm of your hand.
Side Man	: I will uproot the tree of progress and offer you the same.
Own Man	: I will show you the 'path of progress. I will help the commoners to walk on the cemented and coal tar roads.
Middle Man	: I will do this.
Side Man	: I will do that.
Front Man	: This country is of the farmers and workers, for the farmers and workers, and by the farmers and workers. The leader in power today will be out of

it tomorrow. However, the country is theirs and will be theirs only. They are the real backbone of the country. That day, Gopabandu said,

"Let my body mingle with the soil of this country,

Let the people of the country walk upon it."

Side Man	: The farmers and workers are the country's natural rulers.
Own Man	: Leader, Minister and the Government are the rubber stamps only!
Middle Man	: The farmers and workers actually hold the country's reins genuinely. They can tighten at any moment to harness the same.
Side Man	: The teeth of the leaders and ministers can be shaken and removed.
	(The Wretched Man looks at them shocked. He does not have time to say anything.)
Middle Man	: Pradhane! Are you surprised at us? Don't you understand anything? Or is there something else?
Wretched Man	: (He is nodding his head to deny.)
Side Man	: Babu, Our Babu…Mohapatrababu…! He has given five hundred rupees to the Women's Committee. (Woman laughs.)
Own Man	: He has also donated to the Library. (Wretched Man becomes happy.)

Middle Man	: He will donate to the celebration of *Thakaurani Jatra*. (Local Festival)
Side Man	: We leave now. We have to campaign door to door. Yes, you are our people. You will help our Babu win.
Own Man	: If you convinced some older men and women of this village-
Middle Man	: Can't you manage?
Side Man	: Your luck would be changed!
Own Man	: Your condition would be changed!
Middle Man	: Overnight, you would have been transformed!
Front Man	: Pradhane! Will you remember us?

[Wretched Man or Woman looks at them.]

Side Man	: Why don't you say anything?
Own Man	: If you don't say, how will we leave?
Middle Man	: Pradhane! Have you remembered Mohapatrababu's mark?
Side Man	: You will pick up the stamp softly and stamp it heavily. Yes, the paper should not be torn apart. (Smiling)
Front Man	: Why late? Give him.
Middle Man	: Take it… It's the *mahaprasad* of Lord Jagannath. Touch it to your head…
Side Man	: What are you saying? Touch it. (To Own Man)

[Own Man helps the *mahaprasad* touch Wretched Man's head and Woman's head and gives her.]

Own Man	: You are of our religion since this day!
Middle Man	: Yes, hear. While convincing the older men and women, you will give them *mahaprasad* and help them understand.
Front Man	: Pradhane! I leave now. If I were a minister, I would open my door 24x7 for you. Whenever you want, you can come…
Middle Man	: You will sit.
Side Man	: You will eat.
Own Man	: You will hear-
Middle Man	: You will help us hear.
Side Man	: Have you understood?
Own Man	: You will remember-
Middle Man	: You will remember.
Side Man	: Your symbol-
Middle Man	: Symbol of Country
Own Man	: Symbol of Race-
Side Man	: Symbol of the People-
All	: 'Horse Symbol'

[Both Side Man and Own Man position themselves like horses. Front Man stands before them, folding hands together, while Middle Man is in a state of whipping. Wretched Man and Woman close their eyes and ears.]

SCENE-VIII

[It's the office room of the minister. Front Man talks to somebody over the mobile phone. Side Man is dictating. Own Man is signing the official documents. Middle Man, as a security guard, takes opium.]

Front Man : Hello...I am Mohapatra, speaking. Namaskar!... Bajodia, O My Brother, how are you? Hey...hey...!! Why are you telling me? *Hey*, you are for us and we are for you. The world was here, is here and will be here...what happens? The police seize your truck...are three trucks full of *vanaspati* (vegetables)? For what?...is there any adulteration of burnt Mobil oil? What has happened? Don't worry about that. Your truck will reach the warehouse in time. No, it's not possible today. If you want to come, come at 12.00 midnight tomorrow. Yes... yes...we two will wait for you. Well... alright...I forgot to tell you. My daughter is going to celebrate her Birthday tomorrow, not alone...with your wife you come. Oh yes, my daughter, Manu, needs a golden necklace. I don't get time to go to the market. Yes, while coming, you can purchase that for me. I will give your payment to my P. A. You will take it from him...Bye...Bye...

[He keeps the mobile. There is a sign of complexity in the Front Man's face.]

Bajodia! There is the adulteration of burnt Mobil in vegetables. The police have seized three trucks. (A deceptive smile in his face)

[Middle Man starts singing a stanza of *The Bhagabata*. He is now under the spell of intoxicants. He is unsteady and about to fall.]

Middle Man	: I do and make others do,
	Without me, there's no other way.
Front Man	: Mohanty, Mohanty!
Middle Man	: Sir! (Nearing him)
Front Man	: How much have you taken today?
Middle Man	: Not much, an ounce. (Showing through his hand's gesticulation)
Front Man	: I will suspend you.
Middle Man	: Sir, at home is my newly married wife,
	While talking, she always smiles a little,
	If you suspend me, she will get lost.
	Besides this, she is now pregnant.
	What will happen to my child?
Front Man	: Mohanty! I pardon you now only for that *the Bhagabata's* lines.
Middle Man	: I do and make others do,
	Without me, there's no other way.
Front Man	: Yes.

Middle Man	: Sir, if you listen to this pauper-
Front Man	: Shut up…often, that-
Middle Man	: I have made a mistake, Sir. I won't repeat it.
Front Man	: I have told you frequently that you won't say you poor. In our country, never was there a poor man, nor is there. Where you work, the shingles and pebbles of that place are also gold.
Middle Man	: Sir, pardon me this time.
Front Man	: Hey, have patience; there will be your turn one day in a lottery. You won't get a place to store.
Middle Man	: Are you speaking the truth, Sir?
Front Man	: Hey, have I ever told you a lie? Yes, say what you were saying.
Middle Man	: What I want to say is- (While combing his hair)
Front Man	: Be straightforward to say. Leave this bad habit.
Middle Man	: No, Sir. In that Block Office, there is a vacancy for the peon post.
Front Man	: Will I tell you about this small post?
Middle Man	: Sir, if you are not sympathetic, my brother-
Front Man	: Well, all right. I am saying Srirambabu, he will take care of it.

Middle Man	: Sir, if I get transferred to that Supply Office, it will be nearer to my residence.
Front Man	: Hey, will you earn the same respect that you receive here? Where are you now? Who doesn't know the power of Lord Shiv's bull Nandi?
Middle Man	: What I want to say is…salary that I receive here is not sufficient for me and my wife. Then, his case-
Front Man	: Who is next?
Middle Man	: If my wife gives birth to a child-
Front Man	: Hey, now you don't have any child. You think about the future. Let it come to the world first.
Middle Man	: Sir, there will be the need for medicines… the need for pickles. There will also be the need for small pants… and ribbons.
Front Man	: Well, all right. I will consider your case. Yes, how many people are sent by Mr Das for the post of gardener in our orchard?
Middle Man	: Three people: The number one candidate has passed the 10th Board Exam. The number two candidate knows something, while the number three is completely foolish.
Front Man	: He is an unlettered fellow.
Middle Man	: He does not know how to read books. He needs to learn how to write Brahma

and Vishnu. While talking, he will often show his teeth. He resembles a monkey.

Front Man	: Then, let the candidate in number three position, be appointed.
Middle Man	: Sir…! (Surprised)
Frnt Man	: I want our people to be the fools like him. If they are educated, our downfall is sure and inevitable.
Middle Man	: Sir, how knowledgeable you are! (Smiling)
Front Man	: Yes, hear. Send messages to A. Mohapatra, B. Mohapatra and C. Mohapatra. You will tell, "There is an emergency meeting." Go to tell them personally.
Middle Man	: Well, I start my journey now…

[Front Man gets engaged in writing. Middle Man reaches Side Man subsequently. Side Man gives dictation. Middle Man knocks on the door.]

Side Man	: Who is there?
Middle Man	: I am Mohanty.
Side Man	: Come in.
Middle Man	: Namaskar!
Side Man	: What do you need? How is your Officer?
Middle Man	: Why do you tell me, Sir? I have told him a hundred times to increase my salary. He is not listening to me and telling,

	"How can I change the Government's rules for you?"
Side Man	: Oh…I am asking you about your Officer.
Middle Man	: Oh…about my Officer! He is perfect. It's the time to earn. His daughter's Birthday will be celebrated tomorrow! You must have received the Invitation Letter.
Side Man	: Well, she celebrates her Birthday on 'Pana Sankranti'. How come tomorrow?
Middle Man	: You won't tell anyone, Sir, even your close relatives. His daughter compels him for some gold ornaments. For that, this is the mid-night celebration.
Side Man	: Now I understand the case. This man degrades himself for money. Very bad!
Middle Man	: Sir, The chair is like that. Once one sits there, he can't differentiate between the poor and the rich, low land and high land, and rupees and coins.
Side Man	: Mohanty! What's the reason of the untimely visit?
Middle Man	: Babu has sent me to inform you. There is an emergency meeting!
Side Man	: The meeting is very confidential.
Middle Man	: How can I know, Sir?
Side Man	: What you know nobody knows in the world! What's the secret? Tell me…who are you afraid of?
Middle Man	: No Sir, sometimes he gets maddened.

	Until he is relieved of madness, his mind won't function...only meeting after meeting…! But, for this meeting, he has strongly warned. Perhaps it's for collecting tips.
Side Man	: We are trapped. I can't guess. Well, Mohanty, Is Sir annoyed with me?
Middle Man	: No, Sir!
Side Man	: What was the colour of his face? Was he smoking cigarettes continuously?
Middle Man	: Yes, he was smoking…!
Side Man	: Well! Everything is finished…! Mohanty, one can't escape? What shall I do now? What's the way out?
Middle Man	: What's the matter, Sir?
Side Man	: Perhaps information of the mustard oil business reaches him.
Middle Man	: Mustard oil!
Side Man	: Did any fat and potbellied person come to your office?
Middle Man	: So many people come. How can I know them?
Side Man	: If that person told him, everything would go in vain.
Middle Man	: Now I leave, Sir…! I have to inform others.
Side Man	: No…no…no…don't go, Mohanty.
Middle Man	: I have to go to others. I am harassed here because he does not ring them. He said, "It's very confidential."

Side Man	:	You want to leave. Well, you go…see what's in my luck.

[Middle Man reaches Own Man. Then Own Man is dozing.]

Middle Man	:	Sir… Sir…
Own Man	:	(Silent)
Middle Man	:	(Touching him) Sir…
Own Man	:	Yes…! Who?
Middle Man	:	I am Mohanty. Namaskar Sir!
Own Man	:	Suddenly…at this time?
Middle Man	:	Sir, are you not in good health? You have been very weak. Aren't you taking food?
Own Man	:	I have not had time since the day I have been assigned responsibility-
Middle Man	:	If you take food properly, your body and mind will be sound and healthy. If you don't have proper nutrition, how will you work? Then who doesn't eat in this world? Everybody eats to live.
Own Man	:	Well, Mohanty, how have you come here?
Middle Man	:	If I don't visit intermittently, I will get bored. Then, Babu has sent me today…
Own Man	:	Has Babu sent you to me? Why?
Middle Man	:	There is an emergency meeting.
Own Man	:	The situation doesn't seem good! Well,

	Mohanty! Was your *Hakim* (Babu) angry at me? What was the colour of his face? Was he trembling while saying?
Middle Man	: No, I have not received any symptoms. Then,…
Own Man	: Then what?
Middle Man	: I have known the oppression you all suffer from.
Own Man	: There is no other way, Mohanty!
Middle Man	: Who says you won't sit in higher position one day? For how many days will you be submissive to him?
Own Man	: If he understands our conditions!
Middle Man	: What will he understand? A hundred times, I have told him to increase my salary or you can send me to the Supply Office. He does not hear that.
Own Man	: When you are, you take care of us. If you leave- who will ask us? What's in our fate!
Middle Man	: Sir, can you do what I say?
Own Man	: What?
Middle Man	: You join hands with the Opposition Party. You will see; you may get a golden chance. I tell you the truth. Think of it once more. Think of it.
Own Man	: Yes, I will try for that.
Middle Man	: What's the Emergency Meeting at this unusual time?

Own Man	:	It does not sound good! Has he been aware of the Students' agitation?
Middle Man	:	Please, you come soon. I leave now, Sir!

[Middle Man comes to earlier position. He comes back to his earlier office. Then, Front Man sees Side Man and Own Man coming to his office.]

Front Man	:	Please, come…I wait for you all.
Own Man	:	'Namaskar'…
Side Man	:	'Namaskar'…
Front Man	:	'Namaskar'…We have to take some strong decision.
Side Man	:	What does this mean?
Front Man	:	Mr Mohapatra, (nearing to Side Man) You know Bajodia very well. Then, he is also our member and one donor too. The police have seized his three trucks of vegetables.
Side Man	:	I don't know anything about this.
Front Man	:	Yes, please listen to me. Please inform the Superintendent Police to release all his trucks immediately. Otherwise, it won't be nice.
Side Man	:	But, Sir. The S.P. of that place is very strong. It's not so easy to curb and mould him. He is very strange.
Front Man	:	Anyway. Tell him first. If he does not hear us positively, transfer him to the tribal area within twenty-four hours. He will learn lessons from the Maoists.

Side Man	: Yes, Sir,
Front Man	: What's the name of the industry? What's decided?
Side Man	: Have you received anything from Mohapatra Group of Industries?
Front Man	: How did you get this name?
Side Man	: After thinking a lot, I finally decided this name. Then, the members of it are all Mohapatras. So-
Front Man	: Yes, it's good. Well, don't tell anybody about your Cement License.
Side Man	: Has the letter been dispatched to Moda Sir.
Front Man	: Let him know after sending the second letter. The final decision regarding that will be taken later.
Side Man	: Yes, Sir! But he is ready to give something-
Front Man	: Meheta is prepared to provide more than him.
Side Man	: Yes, Sir!
Front Man	: How many applicants are there for Highway Contract? Is there any old customer?
Side Man	: Twenty-two persons!
Front Man	: What's the position of Nayak in the list?
Side Man	: He has been rejected, Sir.

Front Man	: What? Rejected! How come? Why has it been rejected?
Side Man	: He sent the application ten days after the last submission date.
Front Man	: So what? Place him in the number one position on the list, mentioning a back date on his application. He has helped us in the election by supplying vehicles, men and money. If we don't see his problem-
Side Man	: Yes, Sir!
Front Man	: Mr Mohapatra! (Nearing to Own Man) Where is the List of Ad hoc Lecturers? How many students are ours?
Own Man	: Your brother-in-law, my brother-in-law and Mohapatrababu's brother are on the list! Apart from these three, four other candidates are also on the list.
Front Man	: What's the position of our candidates?
Own Man	: Position is not good, Sir.
Front Man	: Strictly monitor the Viva-Voce test. Tell Professor Mohanty that I will recommend his name this time for D. P. I.'s post.
Own Man	: He is much junior to others in the Seniority List.
Front Man	: Everything is possible here. Even the impossible ones!
Own Man	: Any complaint?

Front Man	: Remember, "One piece of meat is enough for the dog that barks and the dog that is hungry."
Own Man	: Yes, Sir! That's right.
Front Man	: What's about Paramguru?
Own Man	: Everything is right. We have also received tips from him.
Front Man	: Good! Appoint Paramguru in the Home Department and transfer Reddy from there. This give-and-take process will be continued, and our love will also grow intensely.
Own Man	: Paramguru joined here six months earlier!
Front Man	: Our tenure is also not more than six months. In this flood and famine, we will lose the upcoming election if we don't collect our funds. Do you understand?
Own Man	: Yes, Sir!
Front Man	: Mr. Mohapatra! The paper has published that the locusts are destroying the crops. Any news regarding that-
Own Man	: Locust Killing Yojana (scheme) may be executed now!
Front Man	: Very good! Expenditure!
Own Man	: Only fifteen lakhs-
Front Man	: Bad, very bad!
Own Man	: Sir!

Front Man	:	Let it be fifty instead of fifteen. I have told you that our time comes to an end. The people have been very much displeased with us. So, before that-
Own Man	:	But Sir, if anybody in future?
Front Man	:	The accounts are not correctly verified. Only some people submit or will submit the proper accountancy.
Own Man	:	Sir, you are great!
Front Man	:	Can we arrange a drink party on the eve of this?
Own Man	:	Why not? We are all friends to each other. God has helped us work in one domain and sit together under one roof.

(All three are engrossed in taking liquor. After some time, Wretched Man comes and goes to Middle Man, while Middle Man takes opium heavily.)

Wretched Man	:	Sir!
Middle Man	:	Will it be right? Take…take a sip. Everything will be right. Your body will be energized. You will also feel fresh and rejuvenated.
Wretched Man	:	No, Sir! We are poor. We don't take liquor.
Middle Man	:	What a fool you are! Is opium is an intoxicant? There are restrictions on the cultivation of opium. But, who has denied you to take it? There is also the protein in it…

Wretched Man	: For how many days will we wait? The bag of flat rice we brought is finished. O Sir! Please pay an attention to this pauper. Otherwise, we will die. Many days have passed since we, the two (Husband and wife) reached here.
Middle Man	: Hey, this is capital. In the broad day light, the lights are switched on. Do you understand? How will you know? Even Babu does not listen to anybody's prayer without tips.
Wretched Man	: If you don't show your sympathy to us, we, the two, will die.
Middle Man	: Well, all right. I will send him the message. If you are lucky enough, you will get something. Otherwise, you and your wife will return to your village. (Entering inside, he talks to Front Man.) Sir, the person has not had anything for the last three days. If you don't hear him, he will die. He is from your area only. Both husband and wife are here…
Front Man	: How can I solve this within four lakhs?
Middle Man	: He seems to be known. He has cleaned our vehicles the last two days and watered the garden.
Front Man	: Well! Call him inside. Call him only, but not his wife.
Middle Man	: (To Wretched Man) *Bapadhana Guna-*

		mani, come here within no time. *Hakim babu* is positive.
Wretched Man	:	He is our parents. Who will hear us if he does not? He has gone to our home.
Middle Man	:	Hey, fool! It's not your village. It is the capital. You will see floodlights everywhere. Well, go and meet him.
Wretched Man	:	(entering inside) Sir, Namaskar! I have come. We, both husband and wife, have come from our village.

(They look at each other.)

Wretched Man	:	Don't you recognize me? I am–
Side Man	:	What's your name?
Own Man	:	What's the name of your father?
Side Man	:	Where are you from?
Own Man	:	What's the name of your constitution?
Side Man	:	What's your caste?
Own Man	:	How much land do you have?
Side Man	:	Are you married?
Own Man	:	How many children do you have?
Side Man	:	How much is your Annual Income?
Own Man	:	Do you have any bank balance?

(Wretched Man is disturbed. He is unable to think of their behaviour.)

Front Man	:	The person seems to be a fool.
Side Man	:	Do you have any Insurance?

Own Man	: What's your number?
Wretched Man	: Number...License...! Why do you need all these?
Front Man	: He is entirely a stupid fellow. Otherwise, he could say something.
Side Man	: Hey, don't you know what Insurance is about? If you do Insurance once, the agonies of your life will disappear. Your life will be insured. You will immediately overcome natural calamities like flood, drought, storm and famine.
Own Man	: Don't you understand this? Have you given some tips?
Wretched Man	: 'Tips'!
Own Man	: Have you donated some amount to our party for the leaders?
Wretched Man	: Donation! Tips!
Own Man	: How often have you run after our vehicles saying, 'Let there be victory for Mahapatrababu!'?
Wretched Man	: I can't understand anything, Sir.
Own Man	: Pure Mother Tongue and Prose! If you don't understand this, how can I help you? Anyway, how many times have you been whipped or flagellated during the General Election?
Wretched Man	: What will I earn from that quarrel and clamour? We are the poor rustics. We go to bed after having a little food.

Side Man	: Stupid! Rascal! *Badmash*!
Wretched Man	: Sir!
Side Man	: If you visit any holy place, you have to give the 'tips'. Don't you know this?
Wretched Man	: I can't understand all this. But, all of you have known me. I am Rama Pradhan. Please remind me of the last event during the election. You are all at my house-

(The Flash Back scene starts.)

Middle Man	: Babu's symbol-
Side Man	: Horse symbol
Own Man	: Big horse
Middle Man	: The fastest animal in the earth-
Side Man	: Horse
Own Man	: Our horse…Babu's horse
Middle Man	: Horse can run with the speed of wind.
Side Man	: It can cross the earth, water and fire effortlessly.
Own Man	: The most trusted animal of the gods-
Side Man	: Horse…
Middle Man	: Of the human beings, too.
Front Man	: If you vote on 'Horse Symbol'-
Own Man	: We will fly! Our country will also run.

	[Woman and Wretched Man couldn't understand anything.]
Side Man	: Progress can gallop speedily at every step.
Middle Man	: You won't forget your dear known "horse".
Side Man	: From the teenagers to the older men and women-
Own Man	: Only shelter-
Middle Man	: Horse.

(The Flash Back scene ends.)

Wretched Man	: Have you been reminded of that, Sir? That day, we, the two…
Front Man	: I am unable to trace from my memory.
Side Man	: Are you right what you say?
Wretched Man	: My name is Rama Pradhan…You have all visited our home. Can you recall Aradasahi Village of Bagada Panchayat? Kendrapada District…
Own Man	: Have you taken something?
Wretched Man	: What can I take, Sir?
Own Man	: 'Bottle'
Wretched Man	: I have not brought any bottles.
Front Man	: The man seems to be simply stupid.

Wretched Man	: Sir, have you not told me that day… "Pradhane! If I were a minister, my door would be open 24x7 for all of you."
Front Man	: Had I told you?
Wretched Man	: Yes, you had, Sir!
Front Man	: You had heard me wrong or somebody else had passed you wrong information.
Side Man	: Aradasahi does not seem to be in our constituency.
Own Man	: Our country has no *panchayat* named 'Bagada'.
Front Man	: Why have you come?
Wretched Man	: All houses are broken in the flood. What we received as relief was like a drop in the ocean. After that, there is the continuous rainfall. People earnestly need food. If you don't help them at this critical moment, they will die. They will float on the flooded river.
Own Man	: Whenever sin overpowers earth, the people will experience the consequence of that they have committed!
Wretched Man	: Don't say this. They don't have a house to live in. They have no food to eat and no dress to wear.
Side Man	: "ILL GOT, ILL SPENT" (If you have got something by evil means, it won't stay with you and be spent.)!
Wretched Man	: They have yet to receive the money for

	their damaged and broken houses. If you don't do anything for them, they will be completely heartbroken and drained out financially.
Front Man	: You have much sympathy for them. For that, you have come from a remote village to this capital. Will you stand in the election?
Side Man	: How much have you received from them?
Own Man	: Speak the truth! Otherwise, there is no escape from here.
Wretched Man	: I have come here to make some arrangements for them. I am unable to bear their suffering.
Front Man	: For which position will you stand? Ward member or *Sarapanch*? Speak the truth. There is no way to escape.
Side Man	: From which party? Say quickly?
Own Man	: How many gifts have you given anybody?
Wretched Man	: I have come here to find out some solution. I have given them the words. Please provide them some financial help for their broken houses…at least.
Front Man	: They won't get anything. Get out, scoundrel…!
Wretched Man	: I can't go empty-handed, Sir!
Side Man	: You have to go.

Own Man	: Those have come here earlier on this path have gone away. We know well how you will go. You will teach us politics.
Side Man	: Do you know this is neither Bagada Panchayat nor Aradasahi village? It is the capital.
Front Man	: Alsatian dogs are tamed for the people like you. The Government runs in your name but not for you!
Own Man	: Mohanty…Mohanty…! Send the person back, giving him blows on his neck.
Wretched Man	: That day, have we met only for this? What was the need of your visit to my house? My wife was right…
Front Man	: Where are you from, O stupid? Had you understood the value of ballot paper, I would not have seated here.
Wretched Man	: I had misunderstood you for your mild and gentleness. You are not gentle at all.
	[All of them start laughing, and Wretched Man loiters in the surroundings. Wretched Man cries out of pain and mental agony.]
All	: We are all gentlemen!
	: We are all learned men!
	: We are all Government servants… National leaders…Social workers…!
Wretched Man	: No…! You are all the traitors of the

	country…conspirators, good cheats! You deceive humanity. You are not suitable to be the helmspersons of this holy land! But I won't let you go.
All	: (A wave of laugh openly) Does the man seem to be very hungry? Throw at him a piece of *chapati*. He will sleep peacefully!
	(Middle Man gets frightened.)
Side Man	: (To Middle Man) Don't you need a job anymore?
Middle Man	: Get out…
Wretched Man	: I may die from starvation, but I can't go to them empty-handed. I have given them the words.
Middle Man	: To die there is better than to die here!
Wretched Man	: No…Never!
Front Man	: You will be Anna Hajare! You will teach us what to do! 'Mohanty'…
	(Middle Man starts beating him, while Front Man shouts. Wretched Man cries out in distress.)
All	: (Start laughing)
	(Woman rushes suddenly.)
Woman	: (From outside) Don't beat him, Babu. We don't need anything.
Side Man	: Throw him into the drain after fastening both his hands and legs. Tell him, "To raise a voice against corruption is not a child's game." Revolution is not possible

by the cat…Being Anna, you will uproot and remove corruption…!

(Middle Man starts fastening Wretched Man's hands and legs. Others laugh and mock. The woman requests humbly to release him.)

Woman : Please, leave him, Sir! We will return to our village.

Front Man : 'No'! The person who comes once to the holy place has not returned at all.

(Wretched Man cries out of pain.)

Woman : Being the parents of the people, you are at last-

Side Man : 'Mother' (Mocking)

Front Man : 'Father' (Mocking)

Side Man : Who has sent you to be the leader?

Front Man : Being Anna he will revolt!

Woman : Please leave him. We will never come to this place again.

Side Man : Are you sure?

Woman : Why will I tell lies? That day, you made significant announcements! Where are those promises? 'My door will be open 24x7.'! There will be an election again! Where will you go that day?

Front Man : She has remembered everything!

Side Man : You have to forget all those.

Front Man	: Mohanty, take her man hurriedly… throw him into the drain.

(Middle Man is dragging Wretched Man. When the Woman tries to accompany him, the Side Man, Own Man and Front Man obstruct her.)

Woman	: Leave me. I will go to him. Please don't kill him. If you kill him, you all will die. God will never forgive you.
Front Man	: But, one who has come here once never returns.
All	: Truly! *Hah…hah…hah…*

(Revolving around the Woman, Front Man, Side Man, and Own Man have started a deadly terrible dance as if they were axing her into pieces. At last, Woman starts crying.)

LAST SCENE

[Great Man looks at Last Man. Last Man asks him the questions one by one.]

Last Man : Great Man, tell me now! For whom did you have your 'freedom struggle'? Was it for those who had worked hard to make the land green with corn or for those who had forcefully plundered the rights of others? Great Man, tell me, for whom?

Great Man : Last Man!

Last Man : Today, every page of history is coloured with self-sacrifices of the neglected human race. For them, what incarnation will you take?

Great Man : All the arrows of 'Independence' return to me today.

Last Man : They are helpless. There is no end to injustice and oppression here. The oppressed and the distressed suffer a lot and will suffer. Nobody has removed that nor can.

Great Man : Wretched Man! For this, had I not empowered you with the rights of 'Democracy'? I had hopes that you

Wretched Man : would do something. But I didn't think you would be so exploited.

Wretched Man : I don't want more. I generally request for a half-broken thatched house to live in…some pieces of bread for my belly and a tattered cloth to cover my naked body… I have been deprived of that, too!

Great Man : There lies your mistake, Wretched Man! Nobody gets the right at someone's sympathy. We have to snatch away this from others. You are here reminded of how the British Government was forced to leave the country.

Wretched Man : You have told me, "Non-violence is the supreme religion of life."

Great Man : Yes, I told. I also tell you this day. But what did you do? Being distanced from the primary truth, you followed the empty ideals. Taking your weaknesses into account, they had stepped up higher and higher the ladder of success, standing upon your shoulder. Did you revolt against it? For how many days will you tolerate this? Be conscious of your strength and power.

Wretched Man : I stand nowhere before them and their power!

Great Man : Who has made them powerful? Your stupidity only! In your hands lies their life story. If you want-

Wretched Man : But how?

Great Man	: You have to get up from the lower step. Make your shoulder thorny. They won't show any courage to rise. Throw away the simplicity and stupidity that is already within you. Make your grip stronger. You will see others will join you one by one. You will certainly win the race!
Last Man	: 'Great Man'…! Don't you cheat the Wretched Man?
Great Man	: My duty is over. I have to return. If needed, I'll visit you again. But before that, you introspect yourself and join the Wretched Man…Motivate him till that time, he restores his conviction and inner strength. He will step up. You have to wake him up. That is your responsibility.
Last Man	: What's your advice for Wretched Man?
Great Man	: No compromise, but 'revolution' is the other name of life. Only this…that's all!

[Great Man steps up slowly. Last Man comes back to Wretched Man. Then Wretched Man starts speaking before Last Man says anything.]

Wretched Man	: I have to hold the plough again to make the earth healthy, sound and green with crops.

[Wretched Man stands in the style of Lord Vishnu. Then the musical rhythm of the National Anthem is on. The play ends here.]

END

Black Eagle Books

www.blackeaglebooks.org
info@blackeaglebooks.org

Black Eagle Books, an independent publisher, was founded as a nonprofit organization in April, 2019. It is our mission to connect and engage the Indian diaspora and the world at large with the best of works of world literature published on a collaborative platform, with special emphasis on foregrounding Contemporary Classics and New Writing.

www.ingramcontent.com/pod-product-compliance
Lightning Source LLC
Chambersburg PA
CBHW060617080526
44585CB00013B/875